BIE
7 SES
AND PERSONAL USE

Names of God

EXPLORING THE DEPTHS OF
GOD'S CHARACTER

CWR

Mary Evans

Contents

Introduction

Names serve several purposes and, although naming systems can be very different in different cultures, the names themselves serve very similar purposes in each one.

Firstly, they are the major means of identification and enable us to indicate who we are talking to or who we are talking about – that is they serve both as a form of address and a form of reference. Thus when Moses in Exodus 3:13 predicts that the Israelites will ask for the name of the One who sent him (although in fact they did not actually ask this question) he is asking for a means to identify God. If he and they were to risk their lives, they needed to know on whose behalf they were doing so!

Secondly, names are used to identify relationship. One can often identify ethnic background from a name – my name for example indicates Welsh links. We speak in English of a surname, or family name, which links us to relatives and, in several cultures, the father's, or sometimes the mother's, first name is used in the way that English speakers use surnames. Speaking of 'the God of Israel' (Isa. 29:23) or 'the God of Abraham, Isaac and Jacob' (Exod. 3:6,16), or 'the God and Father of our Lord Jesus Christ' (Rom. 15:6; 2 Cor. 1:3) does the same thing.

Relationship is also indicated by the form of name used; shortened forms or only using the first name can indicate closeness and doing so without permission can be seen as offensive – as in the situation where some elderly patients hate it when young nurses call them by their first name! God can be addressed as 'Creator' and 'Lord' by all but not all are entitled to call him 'Our Father'.

These relationship indicators can also be used to distinguish between people of the same name as can the third main use of names, which is to indicate positions or roles. For example, 'Mary the mother of Jesus' is distinguished from 'Mary the wife of Clopas' and 'John the Baptiser' from 'John the Apostle' (John 19:25; Acts 1:14; Matt. 3:1; 10:2). Similarly, the God of Israel is shown to be quite different from all other gods and can likewise be identified by His activities, as Creator, Shepherd, King etc ...

Fourthly, names are used to indicate or exert influence. 'Name-dropping' is often seen in a negative light as showing off, but the point of such activity is to show knowledge of, or relationship with, the significant person named and to claim something of their influence. That is to say 'this named person will act on my behalf so you need to take me seriously.' God's name is *particularly* powerful and it is interesting that the Israelites were strictly forbidden to use God's name in any kind of curse for personal vengeance (Exod. 20:7; Deut. 5:11). God's name must never be used by us to further our own purposes or to boost our own sense of importance. It was awareness of this kind of strict prohibition that led to the reluctance to use God's name at all, although proper uses of naming are allowed and encouraged in Scripture, as the Exodus 3 passage indicates.

Names originate in different ways. In many instances they are given originally by parents – although in some cultures this may be by tribal leaders or religious functionaries. However, these names are often changed by friends, colleagues or other family members so Margaret may become Maggie, Mags, Meg or Marg and Robert may become Rob, Robbie, Bob or Bert. Sometimes names are amended to reflect a new position or a job: Superintendent Jones, Doctor Anne, Colonel Mustard, Major Tom, Pastor Mbwezi etc and sometimes we give names to ourselves. Sometimes the name is dropped and the title used as if it were a name: 'doctor', 'major', 'pastor'.

God names Himself not simply in Exodus 3 but on many occasions He introduces Himself using a description especially relevant to the situation. For example, in Genesis 15:1 after Abraham has been fighting enemies and debating about rewards, God announces Himself as 'your shield, your very great reward'. But Scripture also records names of God given by people who have encountered Him in particular ways. Hagar calls him 'the God who sees me' (Gen. 16:13) and the psalmist 'the God who performs miracles' (Psa. 77:14).

Thus, an investigation into the names and titles given to God serves a range of purposes. It tells us much of who God is, what God is like, what He does, and how He relates to us. So in a very real way, anyone who takes part in these studies is doing theology, acting as a theologian! But the *real* point of all this is to understand more about God so that we can know Him better. And, as we know Him better we can serve Him better. We can be much clearer in our minds, hearts and lives as to what it means that God loves us and, in turn, what it means for us to love Him. Only then, can we really love others.

WEEK ONE

My Lᴏʀᴅ, my Lord, and my God

Opening Icebreaker

Think about all the different ways that you have been addressed in the last few weeks – either verbally, electronically or in writing (formal, informal, nicknames, titles etc). Share three or four of these with the group, indicating any that you really like or really dislike. Discuss whether who it is who calls you by that name makes any difference to your reaction.

Bible Readings

- Genesis 4:26; 12:8; 13:4; 21:33
- Exodus 3:4–15
- 1 Samuel 3:1–14
- Isaiah 45:1–7
- Revelation 4:6–11

Opening our Eyes

Names are important! Different cultures have different ways of formulating or choosing names but in every case what we call people matters. Do we know them well enough to use a pet name? Ought we to add the Dr or Rev or Professor – or can we drop it? How should we refer to them when speaking to someone else? 'What did Daddy say?' 'What did your father say?' 'What did Bob say?' 'What did the doctor say?' These may all be asking the same thing, but with very different implications. What we call people and how we refer to them matters. One often hears church announcements like 'If you are interested in … see Lizzie afterwards'. This sounds familiar and informal but visitors with no idea who Lizzie is are actually made to feel excluded. They may not know who 'Lizzie Smith' is either but somehow it seems less excluding!

In a similar way what we call God and how we refer to Him matters too. It doesn't just describe or indicate our relationship with Him, it affects it! Scripture refers to God in many, many different ways and we shall be exploring some of them in the next few weeks, but the vast majority of the names and titles used for God are based on three Hebrew words, *El*, *Yhwh* (or Yahweh), and *Adon,* so it is worth starting by exploring these.

1. *El – Elohim*: (Translated as 'God') This is similar to our term 'God' in that it can be used either as a particular name or as a generic term for any god. The Canaanites also used it as a name for one of their gods. It has the sense of power and of separation from humanity and was therefore seen as appropriate for Israel's God, although the Bible is very clear when it is being used for God and when for gods. The plural form *Elohim* is more common. When applied to God, this is used to indicate respect rather than division or plurality – much like the royal 'we' in English.

2. *Adon*: (Translated as 'Lord') This means 'lord' and is most commonly found in the vocative form 'my lord' (*adoni*). It was used to address rulers, or any person seen as having an authoritative position. Again it is not difficult to identify when it is or is not being used for God. When it is, the English versions give it a capital letter – 'Lord'.

3. *Yahweh*: (Translated as 'Lᴏʀᴅ') This is always used as a proper name rather than a title. It is only used for the God of Israel and is in fact the name God gives Himself when He speaks to Moses (Exod. 3). It emphasises relationship and presence – God allows His people to call Him by His name and God is always actively with His people. This name is used thousands of times in the Old Testament but an early tradition developed where God's name was seen as too holy to be spoken and was often replaced in reading by the word 'Lord'. This tradition was taken up in English versions and when you see 'Lᴏʀᴅ' written in capitals, this replaces the name *Yahweh*. (Sometimes 'Jehovah' is used, but this was a late formulation.) But, overall, the use in the Bible stresses that God is a person with a name who lets us know what that name is and allows us to use it.

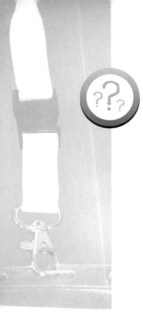

Discussion Starters

1. What difference, if any, does it make to the way we treat people or feel about people when we call them by their name or a title?

    _____
    _____
    _____
    _____

2. Almost all Christians today have learned only to use titles, for example 'Lord' or 'Sovereign God', when referring to God. Does this make a difference to the way we think about Him and is it a good or bad thing?

    _____
    _____
    _____
    _____

3. The Old Testament very often uses the three words (*Elohim*, *Adon*, *Yahweh*) in combination or interchangeably. Does this mean that it doesn't really matter what we call God?

    _____
    _____
    _____
    _____

4. *Elohim* stresses God's power and holiness. What names or titles might we use in English to bring this out?

    _____
    _____
    _____
    _____

5. *Adoni* stresses God's authority over us. What names or titles might we use in English to express this?

_____

_____

_____

_____

6. *Yahweh* stresses God's personality and His relationship with us. What names or titles might we use in English to bring this out?

_____

_____

_____

_____

7. Does what we call God really make any difference to our relationship with Him?

_____

_____

_____

_____

8. Another tradition that has developed over the years (and is adhered to in these notes) is to capitalise pronouns referring to God – eg 'Him' and 'He'. Is this a helpful or unhelpful tradition?

_____

_____

_____

_____

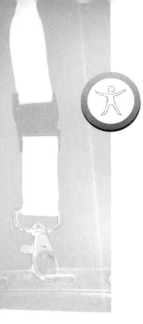

Personal Application

One way of distinguishing between knowing *about* a person (perhaps someone famous or well-known in your circles) and really *knowing* them is whether, when your name is mentioned, they will know who you are. It gives a really good feeling when an old teacher or someone we knew in the past remembers our name. The Bible is full of verses where God speaks to people by name (Isa. 43:1; 45:3–4). Search out some of the places where God uses people's names, eg Hagar, Samuel, Mary. Take time to reflect on how it makes you feel that God actually *knows* you. He knows all about you, He knows and uses your name. How do you think it makes God feel when you know Him and call Him by name? When you pray, stop for a moment to think about what the name you are using tells you about God.

Seeing Jesus in the Scriptures

Philippians 2:10 tells us that, 'at the name of Jesus every knee should bow'. Isaiah 45:23 tells us that 'every knee will bow' before the LORD (*Yahweh*). When the Old Testament speaks of God we normally assume that it is referring to God the Father. Should we be thinking in more Trinitarian terms? Have the names used for God got anything to teach us about God the Son or should we just look to the New Testament for that kind of knowledge?

WEEK TWO

Names Relating to God's Character

Opening Icebreaker

We often hear of nicknames that tell us something about the person concerned – eg 'the mouth', 'the gentle giant'. Let everyone share with the group the aspect of their character that they would most like to be known by and the one that they think they are most likely to actually be known by. Give the group 60 seconds to invent a new nickname for each person.

Bible Readings

- Psalm 7:9–11; Isaiah 24:16
- Isaiah 29:19–24; 30:18
- 1 Corinthians 1:9
- Galatians 5:22–23
- 1 John 4:16; Psalm 142:1–2; Revelation 21:6

Opening Our Eyes

As a child (and since then too!) I was full of questions – the number of 'but why?'s was unending. I didn't intend to cause any offence; it was just that I was interested in everything. But I was aware that a number of people saw this as a sign of deliberate awkwardness. Most of us at some stage in our lives have the experience of being misunderstood. And it is not a good experience.

The Bible is very clear that there is no way that we are going to be able to fully understand God. But it is equally clear that He really wants us to know *who* He is and that it matters to Him that we appreciate and understand His character. We may not be able to grasp it completely but He too does not like to be misunderstood. Perhaps that is part of the reason why there are so many references to God's character within His Word. And many of those references are tied up with what He is called. For example, the 'name' of *Yahweh* is often used as synonymous for *Yahweh* Himself (eg Deut. 12:5,11,21; 26:2; 1 Kings 11:36). Perhaps that is why the distinction between names for God and descriptions of God is quite blurred. Calling God 'the Faithful One' and saying 'God is faithful' are different ways of expressing the same idea.

Today's readings picked out some of the elements of God's nature that are turned into names – He is righteous, holy, just, faithful and loving – as well as reflecting all the different aspects found in Paul's description of the fruit of the Spirit in Galatians 5. Often the names given to God reflect the particular circumstances of the one giving the name – Hagar, for example, calls Him 'the One who Sees me' because of His knowledge and understanding of her situation (Gen. 16:13).

We could spend a whole session looking at any one of these characteristics and there are so many more that we could mention – including God's mercy and graciousness, wisdom, knowledge and insight etc. If we are to know God, relate to God and serve God then it is important that we consider each of these aspects of God; none of them tell us everything about Him, but all of them tell us something. They are not independent of each other: 'the God of Mercy' does not stop being 'the Righteous One', and 'the God who is so Angered by Injustice' does not stop being 'the God of Love'.

We have space here to consider only one aspect, so let's look at God's faithfulness. There is no adequate English alternative to the Hebrew *chesed* which is sometimes also translated as 'steadfast love', or 'loving kindness' (Deut. 5:10; 7:9,12; Psa. 5:7; 57:3; 89:33). It combines the idea of faithfulness, loyalty and total dependability, with that of loving concern leading to active help. It describes the bond between two covenant partners – as with David and Jonathan (1 Sam. 20:8–14). Israel could appeal to God's *chesed* because of His covenant with them. The idea of the constancy of God's help does not exclude the possibility of punishment as, when this is used to restore the broken covenant, it can be seen as an application of *chesed*. Similarly, the continuation of God's 'steadfast love' when Israel breaks faith with Him shows His mercy and grace – as we see in Hosea chapter 2. When we speak to our 'faithful' God it is worth pondering on what that actually means for us.

Discussion Starters

1. When you are praying, how do you decide what name you are going to call God, a) in private and b) in public? Do you always use the same name?

2. Why do you think there are so many ways to describe and name God in the Bible?

3. Are there any names of God or aspects of His character that you don't ever use? Why do you think this might be?

4. How do you think your prayer would develop if you began by describing God as: a) The Glorious and Awesome One? b) The Merciful and Gracious One? c) The Holy and Righteous One? d) The One who is Angered by Injustice?

5. Consider the names for God that you remember being used in the last service you attended. What elements of God's character were being emphasised? Do you think congregations generally are receiving a full understanding of God as He reveals Himself in Scripture?

_____

_____

_____

_____

_____

6. Try spending the final minutes of your time together in prayer – with each person addressing God in a different way.

_____

_____

_____

_____

_____

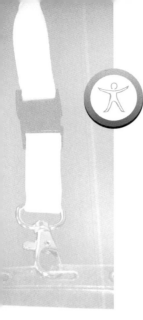

Personal Application

Different names for God tend to be concentrated in different sections of the Bible. This means that if you spend most of your time in only a few books, eg if you almost always read from the Psalms or the New Testament, then your knowledge of God is bound to be much more limited than it needs to be. God wants us to know Him as He is, which means taking seriously all the different things He has revealed about Himself. Over the next year why not try reading a different book of the Bible each month (or maybe even each week!) looking out for the different names for God that are used and reflecting on what that tells you about God and how that might develop or even change the understanding you started with. Each time you come across a new name, use it to say a few words to God. An alternative way of doing this would be to use daily reading material – like the one-year *Cover to Cover Complete* Bible reading guide – and apply this exercise to it.

Seeing Jesus in the Scriptures

Jesus said to Philip, 'Anyone who has seen me has seen the Father' (John 14:9). Think about how the characteristics of God seen in the names that we have considered today can be seen reflected in the life of Jesus. Are there any other characteristics of Jesus that could be used to formulate different names for God?

WEEK THREE

Names Relating to God's Roles and Actions: Part 1

Opening Icebreaker

Talk about all the names that you can think of where the name of the person relates to the job they do (eg Mr Bun the Baker). Give a name to each person in the group relating either to their job or to something they are known for in the church (eg Harry the handshaker, or Frances the fresh-air fiend).

Bible Readings

- Psalms 8; 95
- Numbers 23:21; Judges 8:23; Psalm 10:16; Isaiah 33:22; 1 Timothy 1:17; Revelation 15:3
- John 20:17; James 1:27

Opening Our Eyes

Just as with the different characteristics of God, we cannot and must not see the functions of God and tasks He undertakes as separate and unconnected. One of the most significant verses in the Old Testament is Deuteronomy 6:4: 'Hear O Israel; The LORD our God, the LORD is one.' Any name or title that emphasises one element, or even several elements, of God's work can only ever be an imperfect illustration. That being said, the Bible is full of these different descriptions of the roles that God takes on and we are encouraged to think of Him in these ways. Over the next two weeks we will reflect on just a few of the more common ones.

Creator:
There is not as much stress on God as Creator as one might perhaps expect. In the Old Testament, outside of Genesis 1–2, it is spoken of explicitly only in a few psalms, Isaiah 40–55 and parts of Jeremiah. Nevertheless it is taken for granted at every stage. God is the one who created all things and all people and who therefore has the right to hold people accountable for all that they do and to demand care of His creation. If our recognition and naming of God as our creator is to have any meaning then it must make a difference to the way that we live our lives each day.

Sustainer and Maintainer:
God is also presented as the Lord of nature and the Lord of history who governs and maintains His creation. Without His active and continuous participation neither God's people nor the world itself could stand. He keeps us going, as individuals, as the Church and as a world. As Jesus puts it 'My Father is always at his work' (John 5:17) – even on the Sabbath! God is thinking of us all the time – are we thinking of Him too or do we name Him as preserver of the world only on Sundays?

Father:

This is brought into prominence in the New Testament. In the Old Testament it is not used as a personal address to God and is usually applied to *Yahweh* by Himself rather than by Israel. But Jesus made it clear that this is not only an appropriate way to describe God, but also to address Him. He is *our* Father. The relationship between God and His own people is as real as that between a parent and a child.

King:

As a title for God, this was not used by the earlier prophets – perhaps because of the danger of confusion with ideas of the surrounding nations of the time where ordinary kings were thought of as gods, or else were often known as arbitrary tyrants. It is interesting that names are used in different ways at different times. Again in the early days the word 'baal' which simply meant 'lord' was used for God Himself, as in Hosea 2:16 (translated in the NIV as 'my master'). But, as the influence of the Baal cult grew it ceased to be harmless and was dropped like a hot brick even from human names (so Merib-Baal, 1 Chron. 8:34, became Mephibosheth, 2 Sam. 9:6). But once the possibility of misunderstanding had gone, 'King' once more became a really positive way of addressing God. He is the Sovereign Lord, not only of Israel but of the whole world. He really is 'King of kings and Lord of lords' (1 Tim. 6:15).

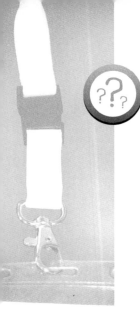

Discussion Starters

1. When you think about God, are you more likely to do so in terms of His character, or in terms of His roles and activities?

_____

_____

_____

_____

2. What difference should and does it make to our daily lives if we believe that the world was created by God?

_____

_____

_____

_____

3. Talk about what God is doing at this precise moment in His role as sustainer of the universe. Take time to stop for a minute and give thanks.

_____

_____

4. In what ways might you and have you experienced the fatherhood of God in your life?

_____

_____

_____

_____

5. How would you explain God as Father to those whose understanding of a father's role is very negative?

_____

_____

_____

_____

_____

6. How does the fact that God is King affect the way we view the world? Does it influence the way we think, for example, of the superpowers of the world, or of the actions of extremists and terrorists?

_____

_____

_____

_____

_____

7. How do people think about kings in today's world? How far is this still a useful title to use for God and how far could it lead to misunderstanding? Can you think of any helpful alternative names that would convey the same truth?

_____

_____

_____

_____

_____

Personal Application

Sometimes we think of God's roles only in relation to the whole world but they are also relevant to us as individuals. These are not just names given to God; they convey a dynamic reality. God created me, God sustains me, God is my Father, God is my King. But it really is important that we then ask ourselves the 'so what' questions. How does this affect how I feel, ie that I am treasured, loved, cared for and protected in the way these names indicate? But also how does it affect my behaviour? There are certainly things we would not consider doing if our parents or even the leaders and monarchs of our nations were around and things we would be glad to do for them. Are we similarly affected by the presence of God?

On the other hand, if you always think of God's roles in relation to you personally then it is important to also work out how His creation, kingship and fatherhood of the whole community should affect the way you relate to people and the world.

Seeing Jesus in the Scriptures

The New Testament (eg John 1) makes it clear that Jesus was and is involved in creation. It also regularly uses royal terminology when referring to Him. Jesus is united and identified with God the Father but they are not identical. He is appropriately the Son alongside the Father. But what does His sonship tell us about the fatherhood of God and would it ever be appropriate to think of Jesus, too, in terms of fatherhood?

WEEK FOUR

Names Relating to God's Roles and Actions: Part 2

Opening Icebreaker

Label half the group 'useful' and the other half 'unusual'. Let everyone choose a job matching their label and act it out so that others can guess what it is. Ask two people to then say in one sentence how they feel about people who have that job.

Bible Readings

- Deuteronomy 5:1–7; Ezekiel 16:59–63; Joshua 24:23–28; Acts 3:13
- Psalm 19:14; Isaiah 41:14; Jeremiah 50:34
- Ezekiel 34:1–16
- Genesis 18:25; Psalm 94:2; Isaiah 33:22; Micah 4:3; Hebrews 12:23; James 5:9

Opening Our Eyes

One of the most common ways of referring to *Yahweh* is as 'The LORD, the God of Israel' (Exod. 5:1), or 'The Holy One of Israel' (2 Kings 19:22, and sometimes 'the God of Abraham, Isaac and Jacob' (Exod. 3:16) or 'The God of your fathers' (Exod. 3:13). This picks up and emphasises that God is a God of, and in, relationship. He created all and He is King over all but He is not in relationship with all. It is perhaps because this terminology is so common and covers the aspect of close relationship that there is no specific name for *Yahweh* as the God of the covenant. However there are other names and titles which focus on the implications of the covenant relationship. God is King of all, Lord of all, Creator of all and longs to be in relationship with all people, but the Bible is clear that not all are part of His people.

God the Redeemer:

Often, if asked to list God's roles in the world, today's Christians put God as creator at the top – it is the first thing that they think of. However the Bible concentrates much more on God as redeemer or saviour. Israel's knowledge of God began with the fact that He delivered them from Egypt and constantly delivered them and sent deliverers for them. He is the Redeeming One, the Living God revealed in history. He can use the world to serve His saving purposes because it is His world. So God as redeemer and God as creator are linked.

God the Shepherd:

Another link is with the commonly used picture of God as shepherd. He cares for, rescues and supports His people like a shepherd. The leaders of Israel were supposed to care for God's people as under-shepherds, but Ezekiel 34 pictures them as behaving more like butchers, treating the people as meat to be used in any way that will benefit the leaders themselves.

God the Judge:

Many people today are not comfortable seeing God in this role but it is a very important part of the Bible's presentation of Him. It has many different aspects. God cares about justice and will judge between people (1 Sam. 24:12). God has created just standards and both now and in the end will judge people against those standards. The concept of justice is very important. God's judgment is not arbitrary. But human beings are created as responsible and to deny that they will be held accountable for their actions is to remove that responsibility and thus deny their essential humanity.

We need to stress again that these are not the *only* ways in which God is or can be described. He is also pictured as potter, as baker and sometimes in the role of midwife, seamstress, nurse, housekeeper, provider of food, water and clothing, and as mother – all of which are acknowledged as normally the responsibility of women. We must be careful not to put God in a box. The terms used can all be helpful to describe God and to increase our understanding of who He is and what He does. But they do not define Him. He is always greater than and therefore different from our limited knowledge of Him.

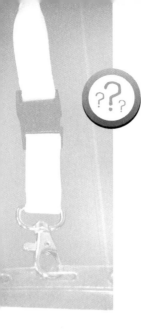

Discussion Starters

1. Talk about how members of the group have experienced God in any of the roles mentioned today. Think about why we may have given more prominence to some roles than to others.

2. Jesus said 'No one comes to the Father except through me' (John 14:6). Today all exclusivity is often portrayed as unjust. In what ways does God's relationship with those who know Him as their redeemer differ from His relationship with the other people He has created?

3. Most people today have never met a shepherd and the role anyway is very different to that of Bible times. Is it still a helpful image?

4. Pick another job, for example builder or paramedic, and talk about how you might use this job to speak of God's roles in the same way that Ezekiel 34, Psalm 23 or John 10 use the picture of a shepherd.

----

5. Should we see God's role as judge as restricted to the end times or is He exercising this role within history?

----

6. The number of ways God is named in the Bible is vast. Using a concordance try and find some others we have not mentioned.

----

7. The New Testament translates names and descriptions of God into Greek rather than using the Hebrew originals. There is a fashion in some circles today of using Hebrew titles for God. In what ways might this be seen as helpful and in what ways unhelpful?

Personal Application

It is sometimes hard when people take one element of our character and assume that that is all there is to know about us. But how often do we do that to God? All of the names used for God tell us something but not everything about Him. Each day for the next month try and focus on a different aspect of God that is revealed in the names and titles used for Him in the Bible. But remember that God is One so, one day a week – perhaps on Sunday – ponder on how the different aspects all tie in together and revel in the fact that He is present with you and really wants you to know Him and relate to Him. It is important that we get to know God as He has revealed Himself to be and *not* as we think we would like Him to be! He is, of course, personal and not just a collection of names and attributes.

Seeing Jesus in the Scriptures

When we speak of the Good Shepherd and the Saviour our minds almost always go first to Jesus, but the Old Testament has many references to God using these terms and ideas. Thinking about this adds depth to our understanding of what Jesus meant when He said 'I and the Father are one' (John 10:30) and helps us to know more of both the Father and the Son.

WEEK FIVE

Pictures of God:
Visible and Verbal

Opening Icebreaker

Think of a car, an animal or a bird that you think could be used to represent each member of the group. Choose one of these for each person and briefly discuss why you think that it may or may not fit them.

Bible Readings

- Exodus 19:10–25
- 1 Kings 19:10–13
- Genesis 16:7–14
- Isaiah 6:1–13
- John 14:8–14

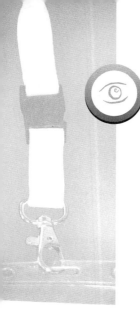

Opening Our Eyes

We have already noted that the distinction between names of God and descriptions of God within Scripture is not precise and that neither names nor descriptions ever give us a full picture of Him, any more than photographs or even video clips give a full picture of a person. They are helpful and while they tell us something about that person they do not represent the person adequately. Having said that, it is taken for granted that God can be described through metaphors or word pictures and that He can give visible evidence of His presence through what are known as 'theophanies', or 'God-appearances'. Of course no manifestation gives adequate expression to the presence of the transcendent Spirit but it does not in any way cause detriment to God's awesome majesty when such revelations *are* given. When we remember that the whole of the Bible is to be seen in terms of revelation it is important to note what forms God's self-manifestation take and what metaphors are and are not seen as appropriate.

In many ancient Near Eastern religions, the gods are often identified with natural phenomena like the sun, moon, stars or streams and rivers. This never happens in the Bible. Such things are always seen as part of God's creation and worship of natural phenomena is strictly forbidden (eg Deut. 4:19). But nevertheless, natural forces that are unpredictable and uncontrollable like storms, wind, lightning and fire are sometimes seen as manifestations of God's presence. They are not that presence itself, but provide evidence that God is really there (Exod. 3, 19; 1 Kings 18). If you have ever stood on a perfectly clear night and watched a storm raging around the top of a nearby mountain with almost constant lightning flashes, you will understand how such imagery could be helpful. But Elijah's experience in the cave (1 Kings 19), where God's voice was heard not in the devastating wind, the earthquake or the fire, but in a gentle whisper, provides another warning not to try and put God in a box!

Again, unlike other religions, there seems to be an absolute bar on the idea of *Yahweh* becoming visible in animal form, although certain metaphors, like God as lion and as lamb, are used occasionally, especially in the New Testament. But many kinds of human metaphor are used to describe God both in terms of physical attributes – hand, arm, face etc. – and emotional ones – love, anger, pain etc. This is usually done to emphasise God's immediate proximity and reality. Another common term to describe God's presence is 'the angel of *Yahweh*'. Sometimes this describes a messenger sent from God (Gen. 16:7–14; Num. 20:16) while at other times it seems to present *Yahweh* Himself appearing in human form (Gen. 48:15–16; Exod. 4:19). Where the angel is seen as a messenger he can speak for *Yahweh* but it is always *Yahweh* Himself and not the angel who answers the prayers. There is no concept of 'the angel of *Yahweh*' appearing in anything other than human form.

Another common term is 'the glory of *Yahweh*' which can be used in an abstract sense but usually describes a visible indicator of God's presence – as in 'the glory of the LORD settled on Mount Sinai' (Exod. 24:16). Isaiah 6 speaks of the glory of the Lord filling the Temple, and for Isaiah this appears to be the normal expression of God's presence.

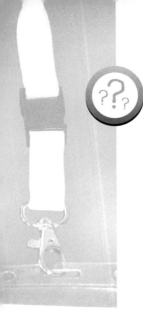

Discussion Starters

1. Talk about any experiences you might have had where God's presence was made clear by something you could see or hear. Should we expect this to happen today or should God's revelation in the Bible be enough?

_____

_____

_____

_____

_____

_____

2. When we speak of God's hand, or face, or God's hurt or delight, we are using human metaphors to try and help us understand the reality of God. Does it matter whether or not we grasp that fact?

_____

_____

_____

_____

_____

3. What would you expect to see if 'the glory of _Yahweh_' settled on the place where you are meeting?

_____

_____

_____

_____

_____

_____

4. Is our understanding of angels more likely to stem from presentations in TV series or films or from what the Bible actually says?

_____

_____

_____

_____

_____

_____

5. Does God send angels to speak to people today or just use His human representatives to serve His purposes?

_____

_____

_____

_____

_____

_____

6. Choose three or four natural phenomena or human metaphors used when referring to God. Talk about which aspects of God's character are revealed in each one.

_____

_____

_____

_____

_____

_____

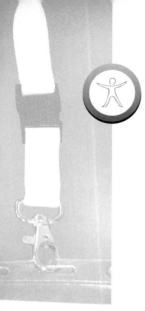

Personal Application

God is real! The fact that we need to use pictures and metaphors to speak of Him doesn't take anything away from that reality. But we are all different and therefore the reality of God's presence is brought home to us all in different ways. However, it is very easy to confuse how we prefer to think of God with how God wants to reveal Himself to us. Am I really ready to meet with God as He is, or only with those aspects of God that I like or that I can cope with? When we pray that God will reveal Himself to us, or that we may know Him better, maybe we also need to pray that we will be open to hearing and seeing what *He* wants us to hear and see.

Seeing Jesus in the Scriptures

About half of the verses in the Bible that speak of 'glory' are found in the New Testament. Sometimes these refer to 'the glory of God the Father' (Phil. 2:11; 4:20) and sometimes to 'the glory of our Lord Jesus Christ' (2 Thess. 2:14; Tit. 2:13). It is clear that these two are closely linked as, for example, 2 Corinthians 4:6 makes clear: 'For God, who said, "Let light shine out of darkness," made his light shine in our hearts to give us the light of the knowledge of the glory of God in the face of Christ.'

WEEK SIX

Like Father, Like Son!

Opening Icebreaker

Identify people you know, or know of, where a parent and child have names that are the same or similar or nicknames that are linked. Where the names are the same, what methods are used to distinguish between the two? Where the names are linked, what does it tell us about the relationship between them? Are both parties usually pleased or irked by the comparisons?

Bible Readings

- Isaiah 9:6–7; 52:7; 53:1–12
- Matthew 1:20–23
- Luke 2:25–32
- Philippians 2:5–11

Opening Our Eyes

We have seen in previous weeks how often the names, titles and descriptions of God found in the Old Testament are linked with how Jesus is spoken of in the New Testament. But it is worth exploring the particular ways that Jesus is named and referred to. Of course the fact that He came as a human being, fully associating with God's creation, tells us something about God, His love for us and His identification with us. Names in Israel were usually seen as having great significance, and Joseph was told that he was to name Mary's baby Jesus, emphasising that He would be a Saviour (Matt. 1:21), saving His people not, like the judges of old, from human enemies but from the impact of their own sins. Names were given sometimes by mothers and sometimes by fathers. The angel in Luke 1 tells Mary about the role her son would have but it is Joseph who is to assign the name. Perhaps this is ensuring that Joseph is fully involved with his wife's son. The rough country shepherds were also told that the precious baby was to be a Saviour, the Messiah – God's promised Anointed One – and the Lord. But in addition they were told that He could be found lying in a hay box in the animal shelter of an inn. Right from the beginning it was made clear that the great glory of God which attached to Jesus was not to be confused with human glory.

The Jews of Jesus' time were expecting a Messiah to come, but they were convinced this would be a great, powerful warrior, who would bring the mighty Roman Empire to its knees and a renewed freedom, independence and rule to Israel. They had not seen the words of Isaiah 53 as relevant to this concept. It is interesting that the terms Jesus uses to describe Himself ('bread of life', 'light of the world', 'gate for the sheep', 'good shepherd', 'the resurrection and the life', 'the way, the truth and the life', John 6:35; 8:12; 10:7,14; 11:25; 14:6 etc) almost all emphasise the providing, caring, enlightening aspects of His saving ministry and virtually none highlight anything related to *human* power and authority. He is 'Lord of all' (Acts 10:36) but deliberately turned away from anything that could be seen as the establishment or human power structures. He accepts the validity of His kingship – it is far from inappropriate to proclaim 'Jesus is King' – but He stresses that 'My kingdom is not of this world' (John-18:36). Paul is very aware of Christ's power and glory but he more often than not picks out the elements of Jesus saving us from sin. He 'is our righteousness, holiness and redemption' (1 Cor. 1:30).

In the end times every knee will bow at the name of Jesus but until then it is the responsibility of His people to bring honour to that name, to be the face of Jesus in the world, to be, in truth, His Body. His power will be demonstrated in our service, our humility, our seeking for justice, our caring for the poor, our bringing sight to the blind. As Christians, we are called by His name. If His name is to be glorified we must show the family likeness in all that we do and say.

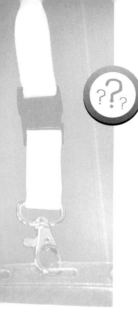

Discussion Starters

1. Talk about whether you can see a difference in the names and titles Jesus gives to Himself, the names the angels revealed at the beginning and the names that other people give to Him.

   _____
   _____
   _____
   _____
   _____

2. Is it appropriate for us to give new names to Jesus or should we only use the ones revealed in Scripture?

   _____
   _____
   _____
   _____
   _____

3. Using a concordance, look up all the 'I am' statements found in John's Gospel. Talk about what each of these statements tells us about Jesus.

   _____
   _____
   _____
   _____
   _____

4. Given the family likeness, discuss how far we could also apply those statements to God the Father.

_____

_____

_____

_____

_____

5. Some ways of talking about Jesus are unique to Him. His followers cannot be described as 'the only Son of the Father' or as 'the one who can save his people from their sins'. But we are told to imitate Him. Which of Jesus' names can or should be also applied to the Church or members of the Church?

_____

_____

_____

_____

_____

6. Talk about practical ways that we too can show a family likeness to Jesus.

_____

_____

_____

_____

_____

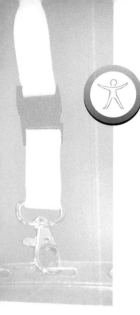

Personal Application

Everyone's relationship with Jesus is special and personal. It is not about technical details but about our brother, friend, Lord and Saviour. Nevertheless, as with any relationship, it is always worth taking time out to think about how that relationship is going. Am I really relating to Jesus as He is revealed in Scripture or do I actually try and force Him into my own mould? Do I think of Him primarily in terms of His divinity or His humanity? Do the different names and titles given to Him have any impact on our relationship or do I see them as something completely separate? During the next few days why not try dividing your prayer time into two and spending one half consciously speaking to the Father and one half to Jesus. Check whether there is any difference in your prayers when you do this and ask yourself why you did or did not notice differences.

Seeing Jesus in the Scriptures

Today's study has been focusing on Jesus and it is obvious how much of the New Testament speaks of Him. However the New Testament writers are all very clear that the Old Testament is *also* revealing Jesus. If you can find a Bible which has a cross-reference column it is an interesting exercise to check how many links to the Old Testament are given when we look at passages which give different names and titles to Jesus.

WEEK SEVEN
Names of God the Spirit

Opening Icebreaker

Think of people you know who have changed their name,
or are known by a completely different name in different
situations – eg Robert at home and Bob at work or Jane to
family and Di to friends. Let everyone choose a different name
and in pairs talk to each other, repeatedly using the new name
and reflecting on whether or not it makes you react to the
other person differently.

Bible Readings

- Genesis 1:2; Job 33:4
- Exodus 31:3; Isaiah 11:2; 61:1; Luke 4:18; John 14:15–18;
  15:26; 16:13
- Judges 13:6; 1 Samuel 10:6; Micah 3:8; Romans 15:19
- Acts 16:6–7; Romans 8:9; Galatians 4:6; 1 Peter 4:14

Opening Our Eyes

The doctrine of the Trinity lies at the heart of Christian faith but one can perhaps understand why, like the crucified Christ, to Jews and Muslims this doctrine is 'a stumbling block' and to atheists and agnostics it is 'foolishness' (cf. 1 Cor. 1:23; 2:14). It is difficult to explain because nothing in human experience really tallies with it, so none of the illustrations given ever quite match up to the reality. It is based on the total conviction that although this doctrine is not itself fully worked out in the Bible, nevertheless Scripture clearly teaches that on the one hand there is only one God and God is One, and on the other hand the man Jesus Christ and the Holy Spirit sent into the world are both fully divine. So God is Trinity; three in one, Father, Son and Holy Spirit. Mysterious, but true. Today's study is not intended to be an examination of this doctrine but rather of what the different ways the Holy Spirit is named and described can teach us about God.

The Spirit is the advocate, or comforter (the word used has both these implications), that Jesus promised would be sent to support His followers after His death (John 14:15–18). He is the continuing and empowering presence of God in the world. The most common name used is Holy Spirit, emphasising His awesome righteousness. He is constantly close to us, but we must not make the mistake of thinking this means that He is manageable or controllable by human beings. He is indeed holy.

The Bible readings bring out four different aspects of God's Spirit found within Scripture.

a) He is the Spirit of Creativity – Genesis 1:2 states that at the time of creation 'the Spirit of God' was present. The word used here can also be translated wind, or breath. Job 33:4 unites the two concepts, and again stresses that the Spirit of God is involved in creation.

b) He is the Spirit of Knowledge, Wisdom, Truth and Justice – He is concerned both with understanding and with doing and is able to support us in our responsibilities both to know God and to act for God in the world. At various stages in its history the Church, or sections of the Church, concentrated on knowledge – as long as you understood and believed the right things that was enough. At other times and places the concentration has been on doing – as long as you show the love of God in your actions, what you actually believe and understand doesn't really matter. A third emphasis has been on feeling – it is really only your own experience that counts. But the ways the Spirit is described in both the Old and the New Testaments show that He is vitally concerned with truth, justice and love. We cannot be seen as living in the Spirit unless we share all these concerns.

c) He is the Spirit of Power – When He gives this power to human beings it includes the power to be a transformed person, the power to bring justice and the power to proclaim the gospel as well as the power to do remarkable or miraculous things!

d) He is the Spirit of Christ – It is important that we don't talk of the Holy Spirit as if He were somehow a completely separate entity from the other members of the Trinity. Different yes, but separate no. He is the Spirit of Jesus and the Spirit of God (Rom. 8:9; 1 Pet. 4:14).

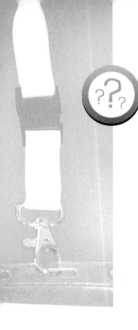

Discussion Starters

1. Talk about the different ways in which we speak of or to the Holy Spirit.

2. Sometimes having the Spirit is identified with having supernatural gifts or powers – does this identification fairly represent the way the Spirit is spoken of in Scripture?

3. What might the fact that He is The Spirit of Creativity mean to us today?

4. Are we conscious of the activity of the Spirit in our lives inspiring justice and righteousness? How might this be demonstrated?

5. What does and should it mean today that the Holy Spirit is the Spirit of Truth?

_____

_____

_____

_____

_____

6. What does and should it mean today that the Holy Spirit is the Spirit of Power?

_____

_____

_____

_____

_____

7. Talk about your experience of the Holy Spirit as advocate or as comforter.

_____

_____

_____

_____

_____

8. How does or should the fact that He is the Spirit of Jesus Christ affect our understanding of His work in our lives?

_____

_____

_____

_____

_____

Personal Application

The New Testament is very clear that all Christians are born of the Spirit and possess the Spirit. However Christians do disagree over what exactly is meant by the baptism of the Spirit. It is easy to let disagreements like that turn into bitter division as they do sometimes. But it is important that we never allow ourselves to look down on those who take a different view from ourselves. As Ephesians 4:3 puts it, we must make 'every effort to keep the unity of the Spirit through the bond of peace'. The question we need to ask is a personal one. Whatever gifts the Spirit has given to me for the benefit of the Church (1 Cor. 12:4–11) and however well I have grasped the truths of doctrine, does the way I live my whole life reflect the fact that the Spirit of God is present with me and within me (cf. 1 Corinthians 13)? When people look at me will they understand more or less about who the Spirit is?

Seeing Jesus in the Scriptures

We have noted several times the parallels between descriptions of God in the Old Testament and descriptions of Jesus in the New. Father and Son are united in such a way that Jesus can say 'I and the Father are one' (John 10:30) and 'Anyone who has seen me has seen the Father' (John 14:9). In the same way we learn more of Jesus through looking at the Spirit and what is said about the Spirit. We also learn more of the Spirit through looking at Jesus.

Leader's Notes

This is a huge area and readings could have been chosen from almost every chapter in the Bible. The notes have obviously had to make selections. An attempt has been made to make these both as wide and as deep as possible but it is likely that someone in your group will point out a name or title that has been missed. If this happens it is worth taking time to look at that name asking the same kind of questions that are asked of the ones that are covered.

There are quite a lot of readings to get through. It would be really good if everyone could read the passages in advance, but this may not always be possible. You may like to assign each passage particularly to one person in the group and give them a chance to think in advance what their passage or verse contributes to the subject in hand. It would be possible for a study like this to turn into a technical examination of ideas but that would be a tragedy. These studies give groups an opportunity, not only to explore and understand more clearly the character of the God we worship and serve, but also to rejoice (or perhaps tremble) at our relationship with Him and what that means in the living out of our lives each day.

Please note that the opening icebreaker for each week is just that. It is designed to relate to the topic in hand and perhaps to open up different ways of looking at names but it is meant to be fun. It should not last more than a few minutes – you may need in some cases to halt the discussion prematurely to prevent it taking too long – and you should, if you can, prevent it from turning into a serious or extended discussion before the group has had a chance to look at the biblical material. These icebreakers are designed to make people relax together. If you have people in the group who can't cope with exercises like this, do make sure that they are not made to feel uncomfortable.

Week One: My LORD, my Lord, and my God

Opening Icebreaker

This exercise is intended to stimulate thought about what a name is and does and to introduce the idea that there are different kinds of names with different kinds of purposes used by different kinds of people. It may be tempting for people to break in immediately and relate this to God, but try not to allow that to happen!

Aim of the Session

The aim of this study is firstly to stress the personality of God. He is not just a distant force but a person with a name. He wants us to know Him and makes us free to call Him by His name. Secondly, we see that the same God is called by different names – a challenge to us not to think we know all about God just because we may know something about Him. Thirdly, in examining the three major ways God is addressed, we discover the heart of God's nature before going on in later weeks to expand on the details.

Discussion Starters

The Discussion Starters are designed to help people identify how they talk to God and to think through some of the implications of this. It may be that people have not actually realised that when we call God, 'Lord', for example, we are using a title and not a name; so you may need to spend some time talking this through. Another example is 'Father'. Many children call their father 'Dad' or 'Daddy'. This is not actually the father's name but they are using it as if it were.

Discussion Starters 4–6 deal with the three Hebrew terms. It is important that the idea that using the Hebrew terms is somehow more spiritual or significant might need to be dispelled (although this will come up again in a later study). *Elohim* and *Adon* can be easily translated but it is harder to do this with a proper name like *Yahweh*. You might like to have thought up some other names where the English translation is different from the original name (eg Joan of Ark and Jeanne d'Arc) to help the discussion along.

Discussion Starter 7 brings us back to the heart of the matter. It is our relationship with God that really counts, not what we call Him, but it may be that what we call Him *does* have a bearing on that relationship.

Discussion Starter 8 should bring out the fact that there is a difference between translation and tradition. Some older people in the group may think it inconceivable not to use a capital letter for pronouns relating to God whereas some younger people might find it difficult to understand why we might want to do so. There really are pros and cons to this and it may be easier if you have thought about these in advance. You may find, as I did, that helpful discussion in this area can be stimulated by thinking about the question (the title of an essay I once read) 'Did Jesus spell "me" with a capital "M"?' Whatever the group's conclusions it is important to acknowledge that this is a matter of tradition and choice, not a question of command or faith!

Week Two: Names Relating to God's Character

Opening Icebreaker

The point of this Opening Icebreaker is to challenge the group to think about what we notice about people and how this affects what we call them and therefore how we see them. There is likely to be a tendency in the group to be very polite about others and fairly self-deprecating when we look at ourselves. If this happens, point it out – not necessarily to change it but just to be aware that that is happening. You might like, if folk are not forthcoming, to ask whether there

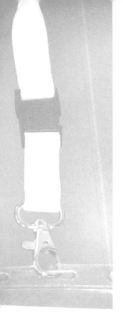

would be a difference in the nicknames you give someone if the person concerned were not present.

Aim of the Session

This study helps us to work through the concept that what we call God affects how we think of and understand Him and that it matters that we grow in our knowledge and understanding. However, the primary aim is for us to find out more about who God is so that we can 'know him more clearly, love him more dearly and follow him more nearly – day by day'.

Discussion Starters

Some people prefer to look at questions where the answers are fairly factual whereas others really like to reflect on and wrestle with ideas. The Discussion Starters here are designed to help both kinds of people. You may need to encourage the first type of person to step a little way out of their comfort zone and the second to be willing to commit themselves sometimes to definite answers, but of course people may be a mixture of the two!

Discussion Starter 1. Most of us never stop to think about how we refer to God or why we choose a particular name, we just do it! But, noticing what we do can sometimes be really helpful so it is worth taking some time here.

Discussion Starter 3. This could be general, eg 'we don't often talk about God as judge because...' but it could also lead to very personal things like 'I never refer to God as Father because...' As leader you may need to be sensitive and give people time to talk about their own feelings.

Discussion Starter 5. It may be that people cannot recall what God was called in the last service they attended. If this is so, encourage them to make a note at the next service and think through for themselves the implications of what they find. Make it clear that if they do this the point is not in any way to criticise those leading services but to increase their own knowledge of God.

Discussion Starter 6. You may prefer to work out in advance what name each person is going to use, particularly if the group is not used to open prayer, or if there are those who find creative thinking more difficult and might be petrified that the name they wanted to use has already been taken before their turn comes round.

Week Three: Names Relating to God's Roles and Actions: Part 1

Opening Icebreaker

This one is fairly straightforward and you should not have too much difficulty keeping the time short. If you think your group may have trouble thinking of names to begin with, you may wish to prepare a few from the traditional British card game, Happy Families. The point is to emphasise that who we are and what we do are not two completely separate things but are linked together. What we do, both in terms of our occupation, but also in terms of much more general actions, *does* say something meaningful about who we are. There is no need to make this explicit but it should in some way raise the consciousness of the group about this connection.

Aim of the Session

This week's study reinforces last week's teaching that God is not just an impersonal force but a person. It also brings out the strong emphasis that God is not just a collection of concepts but that He is living and active. To say God is love means that God is loving and demonstrates that in loving actions; to say that God is peace means that God is

the peacemaker who brings peace. We can never grow in our understanding of who God is unless we also grow in our understanding of what God does (although of course the reverse of this is also true!).

Discussion Starters

It is possible that the group this week will be constrained by what they think they ought to say about God and His role when actually their own experience may be negative as well as positive. The world, as we know it, does not always provide convincing evidence of God's ruling or His concern. If you become aware of this, you may need to bring it up to the surface and make it very clear that to experience doubt or fear in no way makes someone less of a Christian. The need for faith is an important element in our understanding of God – trusting, when the lights are out, that He is a God who conquers darkness.

Discussion Starter 2. It is likely that people will begin here by talking of environmental concerns. Try and get them to talk about other things – eg the way that we treat other human beings.

Discussion Starter 4. People may find it difficult to answer this question, not because they necessarily have had any problems with their own father but simply because they stick to general terms like 'protection'. You may find it helpful to pick out some parental roles – for example, teaching to walk or to swim, helping with homework, setting boundaries – and asking whether we have ever experienced something of God in roles like that.

Discussion Starters 6 and 7. Views of human kingship are likely to vary depending on age and nationality. If your group is mixed make sure you allow those differences to emerge. If it is not then you may find it helpful to ask whether, if they lived in a regime with an autocratic and all-powerful monarchy, or in a republic, their answers might be different. It is likely that thinking in Discussion Starter 7 will be restricted to different forms of government but try and encourage thinking wider than that, asking whether sporting references like 'team manager' or 'team owner' might be helpful in some situations, or ask for business or military alternatives.

Week Four: Names Relating to God's Roles and Actions: Part 2

Opening Icebreaker
You may need to point out here that the second category is 'unusual' rather than 'not useful'! The intention here is to stimulate thought about different kinds of jobs and activities and our attitudes towards them. Obviously it is a fairly subjective assessment as to what might belong in each category because they are not mutually exclusive. You may need to give one or two examples – eg a doctor or a plumber might be described as 'useful' and a peacock breeder or a bellows designer might be seen as 'unusual'.

Aim of the Session
The point of this week's study is to focus on the roles of God that relate first and foremost to His own people rather than to the world as a whole, although again the two categories are not mutually exclusive. The aim here is not just to understand how such relationships work but to deepen the relationship that already exists. The understanding – knowledge about God – and the experience – relationship with God – should go hand in hand. The leader might need to direct the discussion sometimes to make sure that both these elements are included.

Discussion Starters

Discussion Starter 1 brings in personal experience. For some people this is very easy, and for others very difficult. You may need to work on encouraging one or two to say less than they could and others to say more. Often the gems that come from those who find it hard to express themselves can be some of the most worthwhile parts of the whole study. It is important that those who struggle and feel that their own experience is somehow lacking are helped to see that this in no way invalidates their relationship with God and that the expression of these struggles can really encourage other people.

Discussion Starter 2 could be used to stimulate discussion on how background culture does influence our understanding. Some older groups will not see this as an issue, for others the question of exclusivity is vital and the rejection of anyone for any reason is seen as unacceptable. It may help to introduce the concept of family and the fact that although a home may be open to everybody, nevertheless some belong to the family and some do not.

Discussion Starters 3 and 4 discuss the applicability of imagery. Those who have been familiar with biblical imagery since childhood are likely to have a different perspective to those who have not and you may need to draw this difference into the open.

Discussion Starter 5 may open up discussion about what God's role as judge actually involves as well as the timing of it. If it does then allow this to develop but if not, it is not necessary to push it.

Because the number of different ways God is named is so vast, Discussion Starter 6 could lead to extended discussion and you may need to cut it short. There are several internet sites where the names of God (with their Bible references) are

set out. You may like to download some of these lists to give
people ideas if no concordance is available. It is interesting
to note that not all the different lists are the same – decisions
about what constitutes a name do vary!

For Discussion Starter 7 it may be worthwhile asking if
anyone in the group actually knows the Hebrew terms for
'God the Provider', or 'God the Healer'. If no one does then the
question is clearly not going to be too relevant.

Week Five: Pictures of God: Visible and Verbal

Opening Icebreaker
This Opening Icebreaker should encourage people to think
about what a metaphor is and how it can be helpful in
saying something about a person but unhelpful if seen as
delineating that person. In general it seems better to view it
more as a caricature rather than a photographic portrait. It
may be helpful for this exercise to have lists of cars, animals
and birds available to give ideas to those who do not think
so quickly.

Aim of the Session
The aim of this study is to widen the awareness of the group
as to the different ways God is described and to help them
work out both the benefits and the limitations of pictures
provided to describe God. It is important to ensure that
somewhere in the group's discussion, the question should be
raised as to how it should be decided that a particular way of
speaking about God is or is not appropriate.

Discussion Starters
The comments relating to Discussion Starter 1 in the last
study are also relevant to this Starter 1. There are no right
or wrong answers when folk are asked to describe their

own experience. Scripture is very clear that the presence or absence of any given experience of God's action is not in itself a measure of spirituality, and you as leader will need to make sure that that implication is not taken. Nevertheless the recounting of such experiences can help people to both understand and evaluate their own experiences and their knowledge of God. The question: 'Why do you think that indicated God's presence?' is a very valid one and may need to be asked but any critique of someone's analysis of their own experiences will have to be done very sensitively. The group may question the either/or element in the second half of this Discussion Starter and, if they do not, it would be helpful for you to do so. That also applies to the potential either/or element in Discussion Starter 5.

It may assist the discussion in Discussion Starter 2 if you provide some examples. For some people an illustration like 'I felt that I was held close in God's arms' may be very precious to them and it must be made very clear that the reality of that feeling is in no way lessened by the fact that the language used is metaphorical.

Many people are fascinated by the idea of angels and there is opportunity to explore this in Discussion Starters 4 and 5. It may help to have made a list of all the references to angels in the Bible. It is interesting to note that, while wings are mentioned in relation to the carved cherubim attached to the lid of the ark of the covenant (Exod. 25:20; 1 Kings 8:6) and in the visions of heavenly beings in Isaiah 6 and Ezekiel 1, they are not mentioned in relation to angels. It is worth noting however that the wings of God are pictured several times in the Psalms (eg Psa. 17:8; 57:1; 91:4). If the discussion slows for Discussion Starter 5 you may like to raise the question as to whether or not it is appropriate to refer to humans that God uses to help us as 'angels.' Should the term be restricted to supernatural beings only?

Week Six: Like Father, Like Son!

Opening Icebreaker

Answers here are likely to vary depending on the culture or sub-culture of the group members. Using numbers as in John Smith III, appears to be common in the USA as does adding the word 'Junior' although I have only ever heard of a John-boy in the TV programme *The Waltons*! Using diminutives – little Chris and big Chris – or alternative forms of a name is more common in other situations. The idea being explored here is, again, the concept of how names are used to indicate relationship.

Aim of the Session

The aim of this study is to work through the implications of the divinity of Jesus. It is clear that no study of the names and titles of God would be complete without considering what Jesus is called. The other side of this is to consider what the names given to Jesus, by Himself, by God's angels, or by other people have to tell us about who Jesus is and who God is.

Discussion Starters

Again it may be helpful for this study to prepare in advance (or to find on the internet) a list of the names used to refer to Jesus within the Bible. This could be helpful for Discussion Starters 1, 3, 4 and 5. As with many of the Discussion Starters in previous studies, there is no fixed 'right' answer in several of these instances. However, that does not mean that any answer will do. There is much material in Scripture that points us towards or restricts the range of possible answers. With studies like these that are considering broader themes rather than a specific passage sometimes we can move away from the Bible itself and it is important to remember that these are also Bible Studies and not simply general discussions. You as leader may need to occasionally remind the group of that point, or yourself bring the discussion back to the Bible readings.

In general, Discussion Starters 1–3 deal with the nature of Jesus and Starters 4–6 about the relationship between Jesus and the Father and between Jesus and His followers. Discussion Starter 1 could be used simply to ask whether different names are used or whether they can in any way be classified as different kinds of names.

Discussion Starter 2 builds on material in previous studies about the way in which names are given to God. Human characters within Scripture did give new names to God which on several occasions seem to have been acceptable. You may like to raise the question as to whether or not this automatically means that we can also do so. If we can, do we have complete freedom and how do we decide what would be appropriate or inappropriate?

In Discussion Starter 6 you may need to push people to be specific. We all have a tendency to be very general and say things like 'we should be loving' – encourage people to expand on what their statements really do mean in practice, or suggest that others develop the ideas introduced by one person.

Week Seven: Names of God the Spirit

Opening Icebreaker
This icebreaker explores the idea of people being called by different names in different situations or by different people. This is only marginally linked to the concept of the Trinity and the names of the Holy Spirit but it does raise certain helpful questions.

Aim of the Session
The aim of our final session is to think about some of the names given to the Holy Spirit and to explore how this too increases and develops our understanding of and relationship

with God. It further expands our knowledge of God as Trinity, which from very early times has been a crucial element of Christian teaching.

Discussion Starters

For a number of reasons although the Holy Spirit is clearly presented as a Spirit of Unity, talk of Him and His work has often brought dissension into the Church. It is possible that those in your group hold different views. If so then it is probably necessary to let that come out and to make sure that it is what is found in the Bible rather than any previously held convictions that remains the focus of the study. Be careful not to allow distracting disagreements (either with others present or just with different views held by 'others' in general) to move the discussion too far away from the exploration of what the Spirit is called within Scripture. Discussion Starters 1 and 2 should give some opportunity for differences to be considered.

Discussion Starters 3–7 look specifically at different names for the Spirit. Some church cultures tend to put the main emphasis on one aspect, the Spirit of Truth, or the Spirit of Power for example. Make sure that each element is looked at separately but if there is time you might like to initiate discussion of whether your group *does* tend to focus almost exclusively on just one or two of these things and ask, if that is so, what they can do to broaden their focus.

Discussion Starter 8 comes back to the concept of Trinity. Try to make sure that if there is not enough time to look at all the issues, you do conclude your discussion with this question. The understanding of the unity of the Trinity is vital and sometimes the language we use does make it sound as if we see the Father, Son and Spirit as three different Gods. But the Holy Spirit really is the Spirit of Jesus Christ and even if we can't work out exactly what that means it must affect both our understanding and our behaviour.

Notes...

Notes...

Notes...

Notes...

The *Cover to Cover* Bible Study Series

Jacob
Taking hold of God's blessing
ISBN: 978-1-78259-685-1

James
Faith in action
ISBN: 978-1-85345-293-2

Jeremiah
The passionate prophet
ISBN: 978-1-85345-372-4

Job
The source of wisdom
ISBN: 978-1-78259-992-0

Joel
Getting real with God
ISBN: 978-1-78951-927-2

John's Gospel
Exploring the seven miraculous signs
ISBN: 978-1-85345-295-6

Jonah
Rescued from the depths
ISBN: 978-1-78259-762-9

Joseph
The power of forgiveness and reconciliation
ISBN: 978-1-85345-252-9

Joshua 1-10
Hand in hand with God
ISBN: 978-1-85345-542-7

Joshua 11-24
Called to service
ISBN: 978-1-78951-138-3

Judges 1-8
The spiral of faith
ISBN: 978-1-85345-681-7

Judges 9-21
Learning to live God's way
ISBN: 978-1-85345-910-8

Luke
A prescription for living
ISBN: 978-1-78259-270-9

Mark
Life as it is meant to be lived
ISBN: 978-1-85345-233-8

Mary
The mother of Jesus
ISBN: 978-1-78259-402-4

Moses
Face to face with God
ISBN: 978-1-85345-336-6

Names of God
Exploring the depths of God's character
ISBN: 978-1-85345-680-0

Nehemiah
Principles for life
ISBN: 978-1-85345-335-9

Parables
Communicating God on earth
ISBN: 978-1-85345-340-3

Philemon
From slavery to freedom
ISBN: 978-1-85345-453-0

Philippians
Living for the sake of the gospel
ISBN: 978-1-85345-421-9

Prayers of Jesus
Hearing His heartbeat
ISBN: 978-1-85345-647-3

Proverbs
Living a life of wisdom
ISBN: 978-1-85345-373-1

Psalms
Songs of life
ISBN: 978-1-78951-240-3

Revelation 1-3
Christ's call to the Church
ISBN: 978-1-85345-461-5

Revelation 4-22
The Lamb wins! Christ's final victory
ISBN: 978-1-85345-411-0

Rivers of Justice
Responding to God's call to righteousness today
ISBN: 978-1-85345-339-7

Ruth
Loving kindness in action
ISBN: 978-1-85345-231-4

Song of Songs
A celebration of love
ISBN: 978-1-78259-959-3

The Armour of God
Living in His strength
ISBN: 978-1-78259-583-0

The Beatitudes
Immersed in the grace of Christ
ISBN: 978-1-78259-495-6

The Creed
Belief in action
ISBN: 978-1-78259-202-0

The Divine Blueprint
God's extraordinary power in ordinary lives
ISBN: 978-1-85345-292-5

The Holy Spirit
Understanding and experiencing Him
ISBN: 978-1-85345-254-3

The Image of God
His attributes and character
ISBN: 978-1-85345-228-4

The Kingdom
Studies from Matthew's Gospel
ISBN: 978-1-85345-251-2

The Letter to the Colossians
In Christ alone
ISBN: 978-1-855345-405-9

The Letter to the Romans
Good news for everyone
ISBN: 978-1-85345-250-5

The Lord's Prayer
Praying Jesus' way
ISBN: 978-1-85345-460-8

The Prodigal Son
Amazing grace
ISBN: 978-1-85345-412-7

The Second Coming
Living in the light of Jesus' return
ISBN: 978-1-85345-422-6

The Sermon on the Mount
Life within the new covenant
ISBN: 978-1-85345-370-0

Thessalonians
Building Church in changing times
ISBN: 978-1-78259-443-7

The Ten Commandments
Living God's way
ISBN: 978-1-85345-593-3

The Uniqueness of our Faith
What makes Christianity distinctive?
ISBN: 978-1-85345-232-1

Zechariah
Seeing God's bigger picture
ISBN: 978-1-78951-263-2

Be inspired by God.
Every day.

Confidently face life's challenges by equipping yourself
daily with God's Word. There is something for everyone...

Every Day with Jesus
Selwyn Hughes' renowned writing is
updated by Mick Brooks into these
trusted and popular notes.

Life Every Day
Jeff Lucas helps apply the Bible to
daily life with his trademark
humour and insight.

Inspiring Women
Every Day
Encouragement, uplifting scriptures and
insightful daily thoughts for women.

The Manual
Straight-talking guides to help men
walk daily with God. Written by
Carl Beech.

To find out more about all our daily Bible reading notes, or to take out a subscription,
visit **cwr.org.uk/biblenotes** or call 01252 784700.
Also available in Christian bookshops.

 Printed format  Large print format   Email format   Ebook format

SmallGroup central

All of our small group ideas and resources in one place

 ## Online:

smallgroupcentral.org.uk
is filled with free video teaching, tools, articles and a whole host of ideas.

 ## On the road:

A range of seminars themed for small groups can be brought to your local community. Contact us at **hello@smallgroupcentral.org.uk**

 ## In print:

Books, study guides and DVDs covering an extensive list of themes, Bible books and life issues.

Find out more at:
smallgroupcentral.org.uk

Courses and events

Waverley Abbey College

Publishing and media

Conference facilities

Transforming lives

CWR's vision is to enable people to experience personal transformation through applying God's Word to their lives and relationships.

Our Bible-based training and resources help people around the world to:
- Grow in their walk with God
- Understand and apply Scripture to their lives
- Resource themselves and their church
- Develop pastoral care and counselling skills
- Train for leadership
- Strengthen relationships, marriage and family life and much more.

Our insightful writers provide daily Bible reading notes and other resources for all ages, and our experienced course designers and presenters have gained an international reputation for excellence and effectiveness.

CWR's Training and Conference Centre in Surrey, England, provides excellent facilities in an idyllic setting – ideal for both learning and spiritual refreshment.

CWR Applying God's Word to everyday life and relationships

CWR, Waverley Abbey House,
Waverley Lane, Farnham,
Surrey GU9 8EP, UK

Telephone: **+44 (0)1252 784700**
Email: **info@cwr.org.uk**
Website: **cwr.org.uk**

Registered Charity No. 294387
Company Registration No. 1990308